THE FLOW THEORY

Creative clarity through ambiguity and doubt

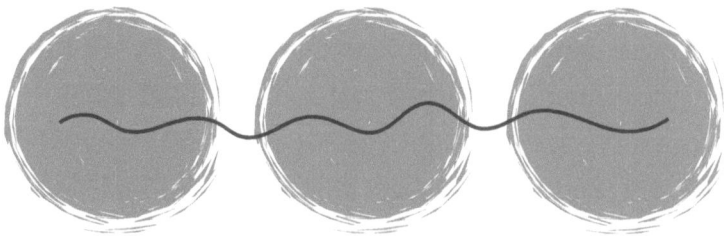

Ali Kiani

ISBN: 978-3-7693-1503-5

Publisher: BoD · Books on Demand GmbH,
Überseering 33, 22297 Hamburg, bod@bod.de
Printer: Libri Plureos GmbH, Friedensallee 273,22763 Hamburg
Cover design and The Flow illustrations by Ali Kiani
Key illustration (Page 5) by Geneo Yunis

To my father, my hero and the best philosopher I know.
To my mother, who gave me the world.
To my wife, whose wisdom I envy and whose intuition I adore.

When emotions run high and clarity feels scarce, The Flow Theory offers a new way to lead, create, and adapt by helping you recognize unseen tensions, reframe uncertainty into opportunity, and move forward with decisions shaped by deeper clarity, rather than pressure.

It's not about forcing open a door you can't see.
Instead, it is about realizing the door was never locked.

The door was never locked. You just forgot you had the key.

A note about the blank pages in this book:
These pages are here for pause and reflection.
The Flow is not meant to rush from one idea to the next. It lingers. It
waits for recognition. It holds space for clarity to show itself in its own
time. You are welcome to write on these pages if something stirs. Or
simply let them be.

About the illustrations at the bottom:
These represent the three stages of The Flow Theory.
As you move through this book, they remind you where you are in the
journey. Calmly, with quiet conviction. Like The Flow Theory itself.

Table of Contents

Introduction 13

Imagine This 15

The Space Between 17

What This Book Is About 19

Before I Knew Its Name 21

Recognizing Ambiguity Quietly 22

The Flow Theory at a Glance 23

Part I Sense 25

Learning to Listen 27

The Subtle Cues 29

Sharpening Your Intuition 31

When the Map Fails 33

A Gentle Reframe 35

Making the Invisible Visible 36

Your Mind Map 39

Mind Map Examples 41

Visibility Through Ambiguity 45

Clarifying Questions 47

The Emotional Scorecard 49

An Emotional Scorecard Example 51

Part II Frame 55

Building a Temporary Structure 57

Framing Tool 1: The Metaphor 61

The Power of a Metaphorical Frame 63

Framing Tool 2: The Language Shift   69

Language Shift Tools   71

Framing Tool 3: Expand   75

Ways to Expand the Question   78

Framing Tool 4: The 2x2 Grid   81

When to Use a 2x2 Frame   85

Framing Tool 5: The "What If..." Flip   89

The Courage to Frame   93

Part III Arrive   **95**

What Arrival Can Feel Like   97

Forms of Knowing   98

Tools for Integration   101

Before We Close This Chapter   107

The Fractal Nature of Flow   111

Part IV Living the Flow Theory   **115**

Misfires and Loops   117

The Sense Health Check   121

The Frame Health Check   123

The Arrive Alignment Check   125

Part V The Flow Toolkit   **129**

Using the Flow Theory in Practice   131

The Flow Diary or Weekly Check-In   132

A Flow Diary Example   133

Flow Theory Based LLM AI Prompts   135

Part VI Held, Then Given   **143**

Reflection   145

Acknowledgements   146

Final Words   147

Introduction

Imagine This

You wake up in a hotel room.
Someone has laid out your clothes for the day. A shirt, trousers
or jeans, a belt, socks, shoes, maybe even a jacket, sunglasses,
and a hat. You put them on without thinking too much. There is
no mirror in the room. So you leave and begin your day.

Later, you are invited to a gallery.
It turns out to be a fashion exhibition, but not in the usual
sense. It is a building with three large exhibition halls.

The first hall is built around different climates.
As you move through cold, heat, humidity, dryness, and
everything in between, you begin to feel your clothes
differently. Some parts are tight. Some feel soft. You might feel
too warm or just right while everyone else seems
uncomfortable. You begin to notice what you are wearing, not
by looking, but by sensing.

In the second hall, you begin to see different examples, fabrics,
colors, and pairings. Some feel inspiring and some are
unexpected. Nothing is prescribed.
You start to wonder how some of these ideas might work for
you. You might feel inspired and even find something you want
to try yourself.

Finally, you walk into the third hall.

This one is filled with mirrors. Some are distorted. Some are tinted. Some are clean and quiet. You begin to see yourself for the first time that day. Not just the clothes you wear, but how they sit on you.

Maybe you realize one item does not belong at all. Maybe something else feels perfect for the first time.

You leave the gallery more aware than when you entered.

That gallery is this book.

The clothes are your thoughts. Your emotional cues. The habits and tensions you carry without always knowing.

This book does not offer instructions.

It offers space. It offers a flow. And if you move through it with attention, you may begin to feel and see yourself in a new way.

Not all at once. Not with answers.

But with quiet recognition, one step at a time.

The Space Between

Over and over again, there have been many moments in my life when logic stopped helping me move forward.
I would look at a situation, try to reason through, and nothing would land. Nothing would feel right.
If it was personal, no option brought relief. At work, the numbers added up, the plan was solid, but something inside me stayed unsure.

I had learned that in such situations, if I threw myself at the uncertainty with everything I had, something would eventually shift. A solution. An opening.
It rarely looked perfect. Yet it felt right. And more often than not, that choice, that leap of faith or gut feeling, turned out to be exactly what was needed.

This happened again and again and the more I paid attention, the more I noticed it. In work. In relationships. In creativity.
I did not know if clarity would come. I just hoped it would. I trusted the unfolding without fully understanding it.

Maybe you know that feeling too.

Maybe you have said, I need to sleep on it, waiting for something to surface. Maybe you have made decisions that made no sense on paper but felt deeply true.

One day, in the middle of yet another mysterious unfolding, a different kind of question appeared.
Not about the answer, but about the space in between tension and clarity.
What if these moments were not random?
What if gut decisions were not guesses, but quiet ways of knowing?

That is when the Flow Theory began to take shape.
It is not about fixing you.
It is about recognizing the invisible structure inside your hardest moments. It is about slowing down when everything inside you urges you to rush. It is about seeing your leap of faith not as a risk, but as a rhythm.

One that begins when logic ends.
One that has always been with you.
And if you are here, reading this, you may already be in it.

You do not have to force anything.
You do not need to solve it all.
Just notice where you are.
Because it may already be unfolding.
And you may already be closer than you think.

What This Book Is About

You may have heard of "flow" before as the psychological state where you lose track of time, fully immersed in a task, performing at your peak. It's a beautiful concept. But this book isn't about that.

This Flow Theory was born from a different place entirely: from the moments where performance wasn't possible. When clarity was gone. When emotions were tangled, and the next step was invisible. When you weren't in the zone and you were stuck. This book is not about helping you do more. It's about helping you find your way through when things don't make sense. Through uncertainty. Through complexity. Through emotional weight that can't be "optimized" or "hacked."

The core structure is simple, but powerful:
Sense. Frame. Arrive.

First, you learn to Sense: to pause, feel, and name what's actually happening inside you without fixing it, filtering it, or rushing through it.

Then, you Frame: you shape what you've sensed into something you can hold. That might be a metaphor. A visual. A contradiction. A quiet truth. A map that didn't exist before.

Finally, you Arrive: not at a solution, but at a shift.
A clarity. A decision. A ritual. An action that feels true, even if small. It's the moment something unlocks.

This book isn't academic. It's not clinical. It doesn't teach you how to be more productive.
Instead, it teaches you how to move when you feel stuck and how to listen when there are no words.
And how to come home to yourself when life gets too loud to hear your own voice.

Flow, in this book, is not a state you chase.
It's a rhythm you learn.
It's a path through ambiguity, one that leads you not to perfection, but to alignment.
You won't always know when you've arrived. But you'll feel it.
And the more you move through this rhythm, the more you'll realize:
You've been here before.

You just didn't have the words for it until now.

Before I Knew Its Name

Over the years, I learned that when faced with complex questions, I had to throw myself into them and let them occupy my mind completely. I knew at some point I would find the answer I was looking for. Time and time again I had to trust my gut feeling and avoid panicking and live in the uncertainty of the question I was facing until it no longer felt intimidating and started unraveling. This has been a recurring pattern in both my personal and professional life: sensing that something isn't quite right, following an intuition I can't explain, and taking action toward a problem I haven't yet named.

Back then, I used to call it my "out of the box" principle. I knew that if I let the confusion linger long enough, a solution would eventually emerge. I didn't know the formula, but I knew it worked. Taking a leap of faith. Over and over again.

Today, I know I was living the Flow Theory.
I just didn't realize it at the time.

Strangely enough, it was the Flow Theory that led me to the Flow Theory itself. Let me explain.

I became curious whether there is a pattern behind this seemingly vague "Question your issue until you reach clarity" approach and sensed that I always experienced similar stages from the discomfort or the unknown to the interrogation of my mind to the Aha moment.

I gave it a metaphor: It feels like a stream, a river.

Then I gave it a name: Flow, and identified the common stages across all the examples I could think of.

Recognizing Ambiguity Quietly

We have all experienced moments when something feels distinctly off, yet pinpointing exactly what remains elusive. It's the slight tension that tugs quietly beneath our conversations, the vague unease that shadows an otherwise ordinary day.

There are also thrilling moments of excitement. Our hearts quicken, anticipation pulses through us, yet we're unsure what fuels this exhilaration.

These ambiguous sensations, whether positive or negative, are universal experiences. They quietly suggest that something beneath our conscious awareness is asking for attention.
What do these elusive moments have in common? Each one is an intuitive whisper. A quiet sign that we're entering a zone of uncertainty and potential discovery.
While we may initially feel unsettled or confused, this recognition is pivotal. It means our internal compass is alert, preparing us to explore deeper meanings or possibilities that live just beneath the surface.

In the Flow Theory, these feelings mark our entry into the Sense stage, or our presence within it.

Here, intuition does not yet speak clearly. It nudges softly. Recognizing these ambiguous moments allows us to consciously engage with what we feel.
They guide us to pause, to ask questions, and to reflect.
These moments are subtle invitations. They offer us a chance to go deeper and uncover the creative clarity hidden within uncertainty itself.

The Flow Theory at a Glance

By now, you already have a sense of the Flow Theory and its three stages.

This illustration of perfectly imperfect circles, joined by a simple, effortless line, is a reminder of how you might move from one stage to the next. Or remain in a single stage for a while, circling through it until something becomes clear. That's why the line connecting these stages isn't straight. But more on that later.

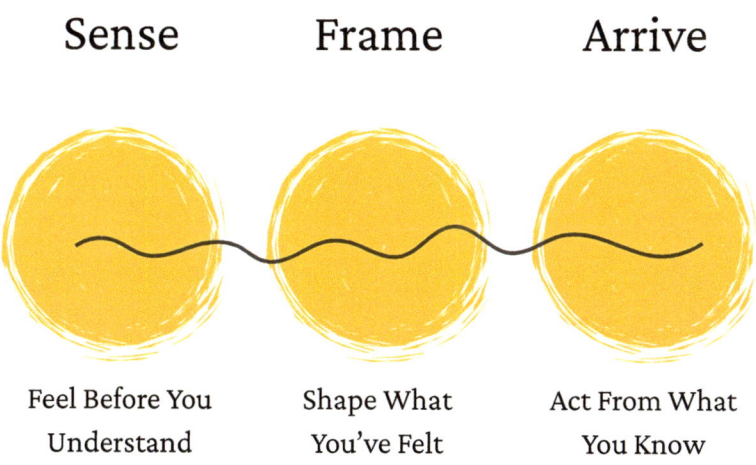

Sense	Frame	Arrive
Feel Before You Understand	Shape What You've Felt	Act From What You Know

Part I Sense

Change happens at the edge of comfort and the familiar.
When what once was no longer feels like home, it is a signal: the old map no longer applies.

Learning to Listen

This first stage of Flow Theory is about tuning into emotional cues. It's about recognizing when something within us, or around us, begins to shift.
You'll explore how to become more aware of feelings, intuitions, and quiet insights that often go unnoticed.

Rather than jumping immediately to solutions or analysis, you'll learn to hold space for ambiguity and uncertainty, allowing clarity to surface naturally. This phase invites you to sharpen your awareness and trust that your intuition, though subtle, is purposeful.

"Understanding and acknowledging the existence of subtle cues, rather than ignoring or rejecting them, is essential for allowing your intuition to guide you toward deeper clarity and meaningful insight."

Before you can understand what your intuition is trying to say, you must first notice it is there. Learning to listen is about refining your sensitivity to internal whispers.
These include vague impulses, fleeting impressions, and emotional shifts that gently indicate something needs your attention.

In this section, you'll practice quieting mental chatter, distinguishing valuable cues from background noise, and acknowledging feelings without immediate judgment.

This mindful listening becomes your foundation for sensing clearly and beginning the creative journey toward meaningful insight.

But not all cues feel the same.

Some arrive with lightness: an idea that energizes you, a curiosity that won't leave you alone, a moment that feels like fresh air.
Others come with weight: a quiet dread, a pressure you can't name, a heaviness in the body when thinking about something that no longer fits.

In this book, we give these two forms names:
When something feels off, but you don't know why, that's a *tension*.
When something feels promising, but not yet formed, that's a *signal*.

Tensions tend to come with friction. Signals tend to come with energy. They both matter. Both ask for your attention. And either one can be your starting point for Flow.

The Subtle Cues

Emotional cues, especially early on and before they turn into clear signal or feelings of anticipation, often show up quietly, sometimes repeatedly, and can easily be dismissed or overlooked.

Here are some relatable cues you might have felt yourself:
The heaviness you feel on Sunday evenings and the quiet dread about starting the new workweek.
An unexplained sadness or anxiety before a significant event, even if logically everything seems fine.
A sudden feeling of joy or excitement when a certain topic comes up, or when imagining your future tied to a specific moment, idea, or place.

These emotional cues, whether they arrive as tension or signal, are intuitive nudges. They're telling you something valuable, even if, at first, it is unclear exactly what.

This is not to say your gut should make every decision for you. But it is to say: don't ignore it. Give your intuition the room to breathe. Let it unfold. Follow the thread. And see what it might be pointing toward before rushing to fix or dismiss it.

Sharpening Your Intuition

When subtle tensions or signals appear, here's how you might begin listening more intentionally:

1. Check in with Yourself
Pause briefly and ask:
"How am I feeling right now?"
"Why might I be feeling this way?"
This simple reflection creates awareness and prevents intuitive cues from fading unnoticed.

2. Give Your Feelings Space
If unease, anxiety, excitement, or anticipation persist, or if you can't immediately identify the source of what you're feeling, intentionally give those emotions space to breathe.

Go for a walk without distractions. Allow yourself quiet time, space, and openness. Acknowledge the feeling gently, without immediate judgment or the need to fix it.
By consciously making space for subtle emotional cues, you invite clarity to emerge.
You're giving your inner system the attention it needs to surface meaning, tension, or desire. This is how your next insight begins to show itself.

As you practice listening, you may notice something else happening.

The maps you've relied on, including your plans, expectations, or assumptions, might start to feel outdated or incomplete.

What once seemed clear begins to feel uncertain

When your job no longer feels fulfilling, even though nothing specific has changed
When a creative undertaking feels forced, like following a script that no longer fits
When a relationship starts to feel hollow, despite no visible conflict
Or when you sense an urgent desire to break free from your current mold and become something more, without knowing what that "more" looks like.

This shift can be unsettling, but it is also deeply valuable.
It's your intuition, whether through tension or signal, telling you it is time to explore new territory.
This is the moment to recognize that the old map may no longer serve you.
And that means it is time to begin navigating differently.

When the Map Fails

We build our lives around maps. These are our plans, structures, beliefs, and routines that help us navigate the world. They give us direction, provide meaning, and create a sense of safety.

But sometimes, those very maps stop working, and the path you were so sure about begins to dissolve beneath your feet. The metrics you used to measure progress no longer feel relevant.

Or maybe you've simply outgrown the story you once told yourself.

When the map fails, it rarely happens all at once.
It's usually a slow unraveling.
At first, there's confusion. Then discomfort.
Then the quiet realization that you're no longer where you thought you were.
And the tools that used to guide you no longer apply.

This is not a failure. It's an opening.

The failure of the map creates space for something more honest to emerge. It invites you to stop navigating on autopilot and start sensing your way forward.

This is often where the first tensions reveal themselves.
Not dramatic. Not loud.

They might seem like the feeling that something isn't quite right, and hasn't been for a while.
There is a quiet panic when the map we followed starts to lose its accuracy. When the markers that once made sense, such as titles, routines, or rewards, start to blur.

You might feel it when success no longer feels like success. When the next step feels like repetition instead of growth. When your actions feel out of sync with something deeper.

We rarely let go of old maps willingly. We hold onto them not because they still guide us, but because they once did.
Because often, structure feels safer than space.

The known, even if uncomfortable, feels more manageable than the vast ambiguity of not knowing, and we cling to maps out of habit, fear, and social scripts.

Sometimes we mistake comfort for clarity.
Other times, we inherit maps such as career paths, lifestyles, or ambitions that were never truly ours to begin with. Still, we follow them until they stop making sense.

And when the familiar stops feeling right, we often blame ourselves instead of questioning the map.

A Gentle Reframe

A failing map is not a failure of you.
It's a sign that you've changed, or that your world has.
It's a tension rising from the gap between where you are and
where your current tools can take you.
This is not the end of the path.
It's an invitation to find a new way forward.

"The breakdown isn't a dead end. It's an invitation to reorient."

Try this:
Write down what you *thought* you wanted six months ago.
Then write down what actually feels important or true right
now.
No judgment. No editing. Just recognition.
This small act can become your compass.

The First Shape of Clarity
You've learned to listen. You've felt the tug, the excitement, the
friction. These were the first quiet cues from within. Now it is
time to bring them into the light.
In the next section, we get to work.
We'll begin mapping what you've sensed but not yet named.
We'll turn vague feelings into forms, and intuitions into
identifiable tensions, so that clarity can begin to take shape.
This is where insight begins to crystallize.

Not all at once. But enough to see your next move.

Making the Invisible Visible

"We rarely write to understand ourselves."

There's a reason mind mapping has stood the test of time. It's simple. It's visual. And it works. You've probably used one at work to brainstorm, structure ideas, or plan a project. But when was the last time you used a mind map for yourself?

That changes now. Because in this next step, we won't use the mind map to organize. We'll use it to listen.

Mind mapping, here, is a form of *visual intuition*. It helps surface what's been circling beneath your thoughts and gives shape to the subtle cues you've been sensing.

But here's the key: We're not mapping the tension. We're not mapping the signal.

We're mapping the space that holds it.

A heavy feeling on Sunday night? That might point to Work.

A quiet thrill when you imagine a new city? That could come from your Future Self.

A flicker of dread before a social event? Maybe it is tied to Belonging or Self-worth.

Your task is not to decode what the tension or signal means. Not yet. You start decoding the meaning of the tension or signal by gently asking yourself:

What's the larger space or container this feeling seems to live in?

What area of my life might this be quietly speaking from?

Where do I keep returning, emotionally or mentally, without resolution?

Once you have your answer, that becomes the *center* of your map. From there, let it grow. Branch out. Freely and with no constraints. Write down associations, memories, phrases, desires, decisions, fears, questions, and whatever surfaces. If you feel stuck, ask yourself:

What am I afraid will happen here?
What keeps me in place?
What excites me, but I never say out loud?
What would I love to feel in this area of my life?
What keeps returning, again and again?

You're not here to fix anything. You're here to reveal what's already there. This is not analysis. It's emergence. You're creating a mirror. One that reflects the hidden terrain behind your tension or signal. And once your page feels full, messy, maybe even chaotic, that's a good sign. Because now, we move from reflection to refinement. Next, we introduce the Emotional Scorecard. This tool that helps you identify which branch of the map holds the most emotional weight.

That's the branch asking for your attention.
Let's start with the mind map.

Main Map ➡ Questions ➡ Emotional Scorecard

Your Mind Map

A mind map isn't about answers. It's about surfacing what's hidden, and giving shape to what you feel but haven't yet framed. Think of it as visual intuition, a mirror, not a solution.

To begin, choose a central theme. This should be as generic or broad as necessary to answer one key question:

Does this container hold the tension or signal I'm feeling?

If the answer is yes, you've found your starting point.
Your starting point might be work, a relationship or free time. It could be your self-worth, your future or health, or creativity, belonging, or even a specific project or deadline at work or at home. It might be concrete or abstract and that is okay, as long as it holds the tension(s) or signal(s) you are feeling.

Place that word or phrase in the center of a blank page and give it space. Now begin to branch out freely and without overthinking. Each branch should be a thought, moment, association, or experience that feels connected.
You can include specific times (e.g. "Sunday evenings", "early mornings") or specific emotions (e.g. "numb", "restless") or memories or flashbacks. Your branches might be desires or frustrations or imagined futures, even repeated thoughts or stuck points.

The truth is, this is probably the hardest part of the Flow. This is where you face your emotions and begin to work with them in real life.

This is where you are honest, not judgmental, and express the vague and ambiguous feelings you carry but haven't yet articulated.

At the same time, this is also where your creativity can be unleashed. If done sincerely, your mind map will most likely already contain the answers you seek.

They are there, even if you can't see them just yet.

What you are doing is actively overseeing the emotional unfolding that would otherwise occur at its own pace in your subconscious.

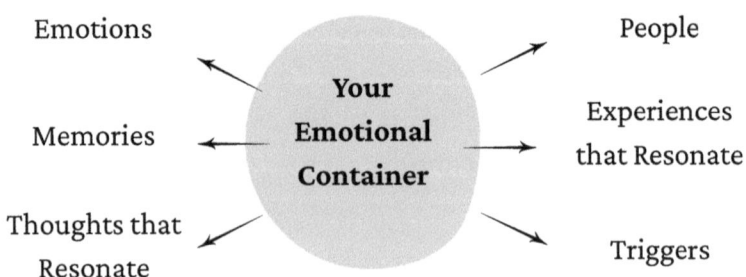

Mind Map Examples

Example: A Shift I Can't Describe

Let's say the emotional cue is a low-grade confusion or emotional restlessness. In other words, it is a tension. You've felt scattered and uncertain lately. You can't tell if it is burnout, boredom, or something else.

You do know something wants to change. You just don't know what. You ask yourself: *What space does this feeling live in?* The answer might be: Something needs to change, and that becomes the center of your map.

You're building a personal map of emotional geography. Once it is laid out, you'll be ready to see which branch holds the most weight and where the tension is strongest. No need to clean it up. No hierarchy. This isn't for presentation. It's for reflection.

Conversations that linger

What I keep Googling

What I wish someone would ask me

Something needs to shift

Roles I play out of habit

Things that make me happy

Things I envy in others

What I'm avoiding

Projects I've paused

Thoughts I'm tired of thinking

Things I used to love

What energizes me lately

Example: The Campaign That Doesn't Click

The emotional cue isn't personal this time. It's professional. You and your team have just launched a campaign you believed in. The strategy was solid, the brief was sharp, and everything passed through the usual approval gates without friction. The creative direction made sense. The assets looked strong. The presentations landed. Everyone signed off with confidence. It felt like it was going to work.

But now the campaign is live, and something is off.

The engagement is lower than expected. The reactions feel muted. There is no buzz, no heat, no spark. No one seems to be feeling it in the way you had imagined.

You review everything. The messaging checks out. The visuals are on-brand. The targeting is logical. Yet somehow, the campaign feels like it's missing a heartbeat. There is nothing obviously wrong, but it is clear something important has not landed. The team is confused. The timeline is tight. Pressure begins to build. And underneath it all, a quiet panic sets in because you can't name the real problem. You feel the dissonance, but not the language for it.

You ask yourself: *What space does this tension live in?*
The answer might be: Creative Resonance or Why It's Not
Landing and that becomes the center of your map.
Even if nothing is visibly wrong, something isn't clicking. And
until you uncover the deeper disconnect, any fix will just be
cosmetic.
This is where the Flow Theory shows its strength: helping you
name the real tension before rushing to rework the surface.

What we're afraid to revisit   *Compromises we made*

Team energy during   *What we Still believe in*
development

Feedback we ignored   **Campaign is**   *Original Idea*
                               not Landing
What parts feel hollow?   *Campaign brief*

Where we overworked it   *Assumptions we made*

Audience Values & Pain points

Visibility Through Ambiguity

Now that your map is fully laid out, you've already taken an essential step. You've turned a vague emotional cue into something visible. What was once just a foggy restlessness, a feeling you couldn't quite name, is now connected to moments, ideas, and emotional patterns you may not have previously seen. The simple act of putting it on paper is a form of clarity.

Often, we don't realize which parts of a container hold emotional weight until we see them outside of ourselves. By giving form to the invisible, we allow unexpected truths to emerge. You may notice a role you've outgrown, a dream that still pulls at you, or a recurring pattern that no longer serves you.

The mind map, here, becomes more than a tool.
It becomes a reflection. And now, we're ready to go deeper. It's time to see which of these branches pulls the hardest.
Before we move forward, we pause. Now that everything is on the page, it is time to slow down, zoom in, and listen more closely. Sometimes what matters most isn't what we wrote, but why we wrote it.
This map, and your reflections around it, are more than thoughts on a page. They are fragments of clarity, shapes emerging from fog. And while you may not yet have all the answers, you're beginning to see the landscape.
You're beginning to understand where the tension or signal lives, and what it may be asking of you.

Now that the mind map exists, it is time for the next step: *questions.*

This next step is not about analysis. It is about deepening and sharpening your view. Asking questions at this stage is not meant to interrogate the mind map. It helps you gently probe, reflect, and expand the mind map.

Think of questions as orientation tools. Anchors that help you notice areas that may still feel unclear, emotionally charged, or quietly alive. A question does not demand an answer. It invites a response. It offers a space for something unnamed to come into view.

As you move through the map, you may notice that some parts feel neutral while others carry weight. Some nodes may feel electric, others unfinished. That is where you begin. The tension or signal you first sensed might still be present, or it might have shifted. These questions help you notice those changes and give shape to what might otherwise stay just out of reach.

Asking the right questions can uncover connections you had not considered. Not through logic alone, but through the act of attention itself. It places you in the mindset needed for both emotional and intellectual recognition.

Use these questions to circle back to your map. Write, draw, or simply sit with what arises. This is where intuition meets awareness. This is where something begins to move.

Clarifying Questions

Use these questions to revisit your mind map with fresh eyes and a more curious heart. You don't need to answer all of them. Let the ones that speak to you do their work.

- *What part of this map feels emotionally heavy or charged?*
- *Which branch feels like it keeps expanding in your mind, even beyond the paper?*
- *Is there a part of this map that surprises you?*
- *What's missing that you expected to be there?*
- *What's there that you didn't expect?*
- *Which parts of the map feel unresolved, stuck, or cloudy?*
- *Which parts feel active, alive, or full of possibility?*
- *Where do you feel resistance, or avoidance?*
- *Which branch reflects something you rarely speak about?*
- *Is there something here that you've been tolerating for too long?*
- *What would you love to feel in this area of your life, but don't?*
- *What part of the map feels like it isn't yours, or shaped by others' expectations?*
- *Which branch could you let go of?*
- *Where do you sense energy building, even if it feels uncertain?*
- *What part of this map connects to a memory or earlier version of you?*
- *Which areas are mostly thoughts, and which are grounded in emotion?*
- *What is this map trying to tell you about what matters most right now?*
- *What feels like the core tension across everything on this page?*
- *If this map could speak, what would it ask you to notice?*
- *And finally, what would happen if you chose to listen?*

Chances are, some of these questions were already present while you were drawing your mind map.
Some might resonate deeply. Others might feel distant or even irrelevant. That is not the point.
What matters is not which questions land.
It is that you are spending more time with the emotional cue.
Lingering with it, circling it, and seeing it from different angles.
This is what allows clarity to emerge.
Not by force, but by presence.

Now, we move forward.
In the next step, we begin to weigh what has been uncovered.
Not intellectually, but emotionally.
It's time to feel your way through the branches and identify where the energy is strongest.
This is where the Emotional Scorecard comes in.
A simple tool. A powerful shift.
And a step closer to naming what truly matters.

The Emotional Scorecard

By now, you've surfaced the landscape of your tension. You've mapped what lives beneath the signal and taken time to slow down, notice patterns, and ask deeper questions.
But clarity isn't just about ideas, it is also about energy. About emotional weight.

There is a good chance you already have some clarity about the source of your tension or signal just because of the mind map creation process itself. That being said, emotions are often vague and it is hard to clearly identify which area is the one that needs your attention or holds the answer you are looking for.
I noticed over time, that there was a method to how I identify where to focus. It may feel intuitive, but it actually follows a scoring formula and that became the Emotional Scorecard.

Emotional Scorecard helps you identify which branch of your map holds the strongest charge. Not necessarily the most logical one, but the one your body, mind, and attention keep returning to.

This isn't about solving everything at once. It's about finding the pulse point, the place that matters most right now.

This is how we begin to move from *sensing* to *shaping*.
From scattered insights to focused direction.

How to Use the Emotional Scorecard

Look at the branches of your mind map. Choose 4 to 6 that stand out, either because they feel charged, confusing, or persistent. Don't overthink. Just follow your attention.

For each one, you'll rate it across four dimensions:

1. *Emotional Charge:* How strong is the emotion connected to this branch (e.g. frustration, longing, fear, joy)?
2. *Mental Looping:* How often do you find yourself coming back to this in your thoughts?
3. *Personal Meaning:* How deeply does this connect to who you are, or who you're becoming?
4. *Energy Pull:* Does this drain or energize you, even just imagining it?

Use a simple scale of 1 to 5 for each dimension:
 (1 = low, 5 = very high)

Now, we identify your entry point.

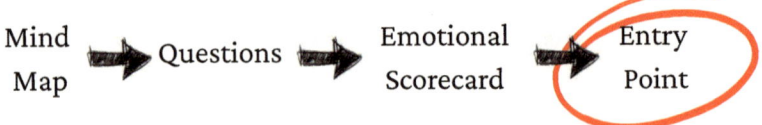

Mind Map → Questions → Emotional Scorecard → Entry Point

An Emotional Scorecard Example

Example: A Shift I Can't Describe

Let's use one of the previous examples, The Shift I can't describe, and let's say we have identified the four branches in our mind map that have the highest emotional charge. The Emotional Scorecard could look something like this:

Branch	Emotional Charge	Mental Looping	Personal Meaning	Energy Pull	Total
Projects I've Paused	3	4	4	2	**13**
What I'm Avoiding	5	5	4	1	**15**
Thoughts I'm Tired Of	4	5	3	2	**14**
What Energizes Me Lately	3	3	5	5	**16**

What to Do with It

Circle the branch with the highest score or the one that surprises you the most. That's your *entry point*. That's the branch asking to be *framed*.

This isn't about solving everything. It's about finding one live wire, one area where you feel the pull of change, and where clarity wants to emerge next.

You might ask, *what If Several Scores Are the Same?*
That's perfectly normal and often an emotional cue that multiple areas are connected at a deeper level.
If two or more branches have similar scores, don't force a choice. Instead, ask yourself:
Which one feels more alive right now?
Which one makes you feel something when you say it out loud?
Which one feels closer to the edge of becoming clear?

Sometimes the answer isn't which branch to choose. It's where to start listening more closely. Pick the one that pulls your attention, even gently, and begin there.
The rest may follow.

You've listened. You've surfaced. You've slowed down long enough to notice what's been quietly asking for your attention.

And now, through mapping and scoring, you've found the emotional cue that matters most right now.
This is the branch that holds emotional weight, creative friction, or personal truth. You may not fully understand it yet, but you've brought it into the light. And that alone is powerful.

This is the turning point.

The next part of the journey is about shaping.
We don't rush to fix. We *frame*. We give form to the tension, not to solve it immediately, but to see it more clearly.
Because once you can hold a tension in your hands, you can begin to work with it. You can ask better questions. You can make meaning.
This is where ambiguity begins to organize itself.

In the next chapter, we'll explore how to construct temporary frames. These are ways of looking that unlock new angles, fresh insights, and creative alignment.
Not to box your thinking in, but to make room for clarity to arrive.

Let's begin.

Part II Frame

There is not a complex problem that you can't throw a 2x2 at in order to find a solution for. You just need to find the right 2x2.

Building a Temporary Structure

Framing is the act of giving form to something vague.
It's a way of temporarily holding the tension in your hands,
without rushing to fix it. You're not constructing a solution.
You're constructing a lens.
A lens that reveals what might otherwise stay hidden.

Framing is not about having the answer. It's about getting
closer. You're not here to solve the tension. Not just yet.
You're here to shape it just enough so you can begin to move
around it, see it differently, and hold it from multiple angles.
You've sensed the emotional cue and you've located the space it
is coming from.

Now comes the moment to engage.
Not with force, but with care.
You invite clarity not by chasing it, but by changing the way you
look at the cue.

Sometimes, a frame will click. Sometimes, it won't.
You might find yourself excited by a new angle, only to discover
it leads you in circles.
That's not failure. That's exploration.
In this chapter, you'll explore different ways to frame the
tension or signal you're working with.

This book offers five distinct ways to frame your emotional cues:

1. *Metaphors* for emotional, intuitive access
2. *Language shift* for shifting the words that shape your reality
3. *Questions* for gently expanding and deepening your perspective
4. *2x2 Grids* for visualizing the dynamics between opposing forces
5. *"What If..." Flips* for subverting assumptions and unlocking hidden paths

Each of these is a tool. There might be a lot more framing tools out there or those you can come up with yourself.
Let's start with these five for now. Some will fit better than others, depending on where you are and what you're holding. Use them fluidly. Test them. Abandon them or return to them. Because framing isn't about certainty. It's about flexibility. It's not a destination. It's a mental practice and the more you practice, the more fluent you become in switching frames instinctively. Over time, it becomes second nature to see from more than one perspective at once.

Often, you'll find yourself using some or all of these frames simultaneously, without even realizing it. Only later, when you look back, do you notice how clarity quietly took shape.

Framing Tool 1: The Metaphor

When logic falls short, we can speak in symbol.
There are moments when no strategy feels satisfying or seems to make the situation any clearer. You've asked the questions. You've mapped the tension.
But clarity still resists you. Not because it isn't there, but because it doesn't speak in the language of logic.
Sometimes, the tension speaks in *image*.
In symbol. In metaphor.
We use metaphors every day without paying much attention to them. They are a communication tool that helps bridge the gaps in common understanding in a way that words or situations sometimes cannot. A good metaphor can act as a compass navigating a complicated terrain or light shining into dimmed uncertainty.

"You don't force a metaphor. You feel it arrive quietly, but unmistakably."

Metaphors hold *complexity in simple form*.
They bypass analysis and go straight to *intuition*.
And sometimes, one small shift in imagery can unlock an entirely new way of seeing.

A Frame That Changed Everything.

There was a time when I felt hijacked by my own mind.
Small irritations, passing tensions, or unpleasant moments
would take center stage. They'd steal my attention, dictate the
tone of my day, and drown out everything else.

I found myself reaching for the *Flow Theory* in search of an
answer. I began reflecting, sensing the tension, and looking for
a metaphor that could help me see beyond the discomfort. It
took me at least a couple of metaphors before that one image
came along that immediately put me at ease. It just made sense
and I was then able to see through the singularities that
bothered me and see the bigger picture. That's when something
shifted.

A ballroom. A grand, open hall. A theatre with a beautiful stage.
My state of mind was the ballroom. And those irritations? They
were just *guests* seated at a dark table somewhere in the back,
but they weren't the hosts.
They didn't belong on the *stage*.
They didn't get the *mic*.
They didn't get to *control the music*.
That metaphor gave me the distance I needed.
It didn't eliminate the discomfort, but it helped me place it.
It helped me remember that not every guest deserves my
spotlight.

The Power of a Metaphorical Frame

This book begins with a metaphor for what it is: A gallery taking you through three stages until you are able to see what you are carrying.

Metaphors are not just poetic descriptions.
They are active frames. Living models that help you see what logic alone cannot.
They let you approach tension or signal from a different angle.
And from that angle, something new often emerges.
A good metaphor shifts your stance.
It gives form to the formless, especially when you are facing vague or overwhelming emotions.

We all recognize the power of a well-placed metaphor. It can unite people, shift entire visions, and make the invisible feel tangible.

In my case, the metaphor I found did not just describe the tension. It *reshaped* it.
Sometimes, it is not the problem that needs solving.
It is the way you are holding it.
When you search for a frame to hold a signal or a tension, what you are really doing is giving *shape* to ambiguity.
You are trying to call it by name.
And often, the name that comes first is not a label.

It is a *metaphor*.

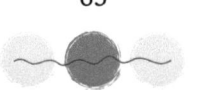

Example Tension Metaphors:
These arise when you feel friction, compression, confusion, or a quiet sense that something isn't right.

Tension Metaphor	Example Explanation
Boxed In	You're stuck inside a shape that's too small for who you are becoming. You keep hitting the edges.
Tightrope Walk	Every step feels risky. There's no room for failure. You're performing, not exploring.
Outdated Map	You're following a plan that no longer matches your reality. Familiar path, wrong terrain.
Paper-Thin	It all looks good on the surface but won't hold up under real pressure.
Sealed Jar	You've bottled up insight, emotion, or truth but nothing can breathe. Nothing can grow.
Closing Walls	Your space, creative, emotional, or professional, feels like it's shrinking. You're running out of air.

Example Signal Metaphors:
These often appear when something new is trying to emerge. When you feel excitement, possibility, or curiosity, even if it is vague.

Signal Metaphor	Example Explanation
Flight	You feel lifted. Light. A quiet sense of momentum that doesn't need permission.
Sunlight Breaking Through	A moment of warmth. Illumination. Something becomes clearer without being forced.
Fresh Air	Relief. Expansion. A breath you didn't know you were holding finally released.
Mountaintop View	You zoom out. See the full picture. Orientation returns.
Beginning a Journey	You're at the threshold. You don't know exactly where you're going, but you know it is time to begin.

These metaphors aren't just poetic descriptions. They are active frames.

They let you look at the tension sideways and from that angle, something new often emerges.

While writing this book, there's been one image that has stayed with me from the very beginning: *a lantern in the fog*. Not a flashlight. Not a map. A lantern.

Something that doesn't cut through the fog but glows within it. It doesn't show you the whole path. It only reveals what's right in front of you. That's what this book has been for me.

Holding onto that metaphor helped me shape each page, one thought at a time. A quiet reminder of what I'm trying to do, and what this book is and, more importantly, what it isn't.

The right metaphor is not there necessarily to give you the answers, but to offer just enough clarity to help you move toward them.

That's what every frame in this chapter has aimed to do.

A soft, emotional clarity that helps you keep going.

Not by solving the whole thing, but by revealing what matters right now. One step at a time.

What's ahead is not certainty.

It's *motion*.

Framing Tool 2: The Language Shift

Language is not just how we describe the world. It's how we shape it. There's a moment in almost every stuck situation where the words we're using start working against us. The labels, the names, the way we describe the tension.
We repeat them so often, they become part of the trap.

That's where this tool comes in.
Changing your language is not about dressing things up or being clever. It's about making the invisible assumptions visible. It's about noticing how the way we *name* something affects how we *feel* about it and how we *move* through it.

Because words carry energy.

A *plateau* might be a failure in one context, but a resting point in another.
Overwhelmed might feel like weakness, until you reframe it as full capacity.
Calling something a *setback* might signal loss, yet calling it a *reset* might signal possibility.

You might wonder how language differs from metaphor. They can seem similar at first, but they play different roles.

Metaphor offers a new frame of perception. It is a symbolic lens. Language offers a mental handle. It gives you something to hold and work with.

Metaphor is imaginative. It bypasses logic and stirs the gut. Language is precise. It organizes your thoughts and brings form to what you sense.

Clarity does not always come from the outside. It often begins within, and language can be the key.

Both metaphor and language shift help you see differently. But language is what helps you name what you have seen.

Take the example of a campaign that is not landing.

A metaphor might be: *"This campaign feels like a dish that is colorful but tastes like nothing."*

The image brings forward a feeling of staleness and lost energy. Technically correct, but with no soul. And from there, language gives you clarity.

Maybe you have been calling it *"a digital conversion campaign"* but what it really should be is something else.

So you rename it. *"A momentum builder."* Or *"a cultural spark."*

With that shift, your mind reorients. The name alone changes your approach.

Language Shift Tools

Although it might seem intuitive, there are still concrete ways you can deliberately and consciously use language shift to shape a frame that contains your emotional cue. Here are three ways I find myself using most:

1- Flip the Term
Take the word you keep using, about your challenge, project, or feeling. Write it at the top of a page.
Now try flipping it:
What's its opposite?
What's a more neutral version?
What's a softer version?
What's a version that implies agency instead of stagnation?

When the name shifts, the meaning shifts.
And when the meaning shifts, motion becomes possible.
For example, "Burnout" could become "Capacity limit".
"Failure" might be "Filter" and "Block" can also be interpreted as a "Pause".

Sometimes, the shift of a single word can move you emotionally and mentally into a different state.

2- Strip the Adjectives

We often describe what we feel using adjectives that add weight, intensity, or pressure. These words are not wrong. They are part of how we give meaning to experience. But sometimes, they cloud the center of what we are trying to name.

An impossible deadline. A once-in-a-lifetime opportunity. A perfect new beginning. An exhausting role.

These are emotionally rich phrases. They carry tone, memory, hope, fear, and judgment. But when we are trying to frame something more clearly, these layers can make it harder to see what is really there.

Try stripping the adjectives away.

Say "deadline" instead of "crushing deadline."

Say "conversation" instead of "terrifying conversation."

Say "opportunity" instead of "once-in-a-lifetime opportunity."

Say "beginning."

Say "role."

Say "project."

What remains is not less true. It is more open.

More available to be seen, questioned, and understood.

We are not ignoring the emotional charge. We are loosening its grip so we can be with what is present more honestly. This kind of naming is not about reduction. It is about relationship. It helps us relate to what we are holding with fewer assumptions. Whether the cue is painful or promising, this tool is a way of letting it breathe.

Removing the adjectives does not fix the feeling. It clears the surface so something more grounded can begin to show.
Try it with a few words from your own map.
Remove the adjectives and let the words stand on their own.
Then listen to what they are still trying to tell you.

3- Try a Synonym Sprint

Look at it this way. The more you look at something from a different angle, the more likely you are to see what you need to see.
Using synonyms and alternative language gives you two things. More time to spend with the emotional cue. And subtle shifts in how that tension or signal might feel.
Naming something as *large* or *grand* or *monumental* helps you hear what matters. And that is what this tool is about.

List five to ten alternative words or phrases for the current term you are using to describe the tension or signal. Do not filter. Just write.
Then ask yourself:
Which one feels truer?
Which one opens curiosity?
Which one makes me feel less stuck?

Watch how your emotional orientation begins to shift as you try different versions.

Sometimes clarity lives in the word you almost *didn't* write. The one that names what you were not yet ready to say.

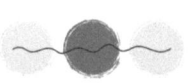

Framing Tool 3: Expand

Sometimes the emotional cue is unclear because we are not asking the right questions.

There's a reason the right question feels like a turning point. It doesn't solve, but it opens.

We often lock ourselves in with the first question that comes to mind, without realizing that the question itself is shaping the tension.

In these moments, we don't need to force a solution; we need to change the question. This is what the reframing question is about.

The Locked Room

Asking the wrong question is like searching for a key inside the wrong room. It won't matter how hard you search when you are not in the right room.

Reframing the question is like finding the right room to look for your key and that is when you will find out that you've been facing the wrong direction all along.

"A good question, even if it does not give you the answer, can point you to the right direction to start moving in."

It is always a good habit to keep asking yourself: *Am I asking the right questions?*

A reframing question isn't a magic wand, it is a tool to shift perspective. And the best part? It doesn't need to give you an immediate answer. Sometimes the value of a reframing question is simply in providing relief from the overwhelming doubt by shifting the frame enough to see something new.

Still, just because you've reframed doesn't mean you've solved it. You might find that after a few questions, you'll discover a better one to ask. That's not failure. That's your mind learning to dance with the tension.
What you are doing here is not chasing the perfect question.
You are loosening the grip of the first one.
Because the first question that comes to mind is often shaped by fear, urgency, or assumption. It reflects the surface, not the depth.

A better question does not necessarily feel more clever. It feels more spacious and gives you a little more room to move.
A little more trust in the process.
And a little more curiosity about what else might be true.
That is the quiet power of reframing.
It does not rush you to an answer.
It opens a door you had not yet considered.

You also need to be aware of common "Trap Question" Patterns. These certain questions might evoke the wrong answers and get us farther from the clarity we seek.
They shrink our thinking just when we need it to expand.

Trap Question Type	Example	Reframed Question
Defensive	"Why is this happening to me?"	"What is this situation asking of me?"
Binary	"Do I quit or not?"	"What other options might exist between staying and leaving?"
Self-Judging	"What's wrong with me?"	"What is this feeling trying to tell me?"

Ways to Expand the Question

Take the most pressing tension or exciting signal from your mind map, or the branch that feels the most urgent. Write down the first question that comes to mind. Then, reframe it. Shift the frame by asking:

"What would change if I saw this as an invitation instead of a problem?"

"What's the deeper need hiding behind this tension?"

"What if the stagnation is a symptom, not the root?"

"What would I ask if I knew the answer already lives inside the question?"

This isn't about finding the right question. It's about making room for clarity to emerge by seeing the problem from another angle. For example, when we look at the campaign case, instead of asking *"Why isn't this campaign landing?"* we can ask *"What part of this campaign are we might be pretending to believe in?"*

Or *"What is this campaign still trying to become and are we listening?"*

Or *"What truth about the audience are we skimming over?"*

Reframing doesn't necessarily have to give you answers. But it gives you space. It gives your mind room to breathe and make connections that weren't possible before.

Expanding is not about finding the perfect question.

Sometimes, the act of reframing itself is the release you need. You're letting your mind shift from rigid thinking to fluid exploration.

Framing Tool 4: The 2x2 Grid

When we're caught in creative or emotional tension, the forces pulling us often feel scattered and confusing.
A 2x2 grid creates a temporary structure, a way to hold two opposing ideas at once, and to look for clarity in the spaces between them, making it easier to spot where the tension is. It creates a framework for seeing the situation in new dimensions. By placing two contrasting perspectives on axes, you can start to organize the ambiguity. It isn't about finding the perfect quadrant right away, it is about exploring how the different forces interact and where the tension is most active.

The grid helps you see what is and what could be, not just what's missing. At this point, you don't need to find the "right quadrant" immediately. Just let the grid expand the way you're thinking.

How to Use the 2x2 Grid
Look at your Emotional Scorecard and the one branch that stands out. Pick two forces from your mind map that seem to pull in opposite directions. Opposing forces don't always have to be binary or combative, they can also be complementary tensions that exist on a spectrum.
These, for example, could be Known vs. Unknown, or Ambition vs. Exhaustion, or External Expectations vs. Internal Truth, or Short-Term vs. Long-Term.
Create your 2x2 grid. Label your axes with these two forces, and let your situation fill in the quadrants. Notice where the tension feels most concentrated.

The point is not to locate the perfect answer. It is to reveal the landscape. You are identifying the dynamics of what is truly at play. The opposing forces. The invisible pressures. The quiet pull between what feels known and what feels necessary.
By mapping the tension this way, you begin to see its structure. Not the final solution, but the architecture of what holds it. This is how you start separating what is loud from what is real. You see where things cluster. Where they avoid each other. Where they ask to be held at the same time.

Sometimes, clarity comes just from seeing it all laid out. The 2x2 grid might not provide immediate clarity, but it gives you a new map. You will likely begin to see places where different forces intersect, and where your energy is invested. Some quadrants may feel familiar, while others reveal new areas to explore.

It's important to remember that this is a mental process, not a linear path to an answer. If you expect a linear path or a shortcut, you might find yourself frustrated.

You might try five different frames. Or ten. Some will lead nowhere, some will give you unexpected relief, and one might just click. But here's the truth: Every frame you try is one step closer to the answer. Even the ones that don't work are teaching you something.

You're learning to navigate ambiguity. To feel comfortable with fluidity. You're building the mental muscles that allow you to move between perspectives with ease, and soon, you'll no longer be stuck by the lack of a perfect frame.

Let's revisit the earlier example where the creative campaign is not landing and resonating with the audience:
"The campaign looks good, but it is not resonating."
We can try this frame:

Horizontal Axis	Vertical Axis
Audience Expectation (Surface needs)	Brand Integrity (Core truth)

This frame gives you quadrants like:

High Audience / High Brand: Where we're aligned

High Audience / Low Brand: Where we're pandering

Low Audience / High Brand: Where we're being noble but disconnected

Low Audience / Low Brand: Where we're wasting energy

Now ask:

Where does this campaign live right now?

And what quadrant feels worth exploring next?

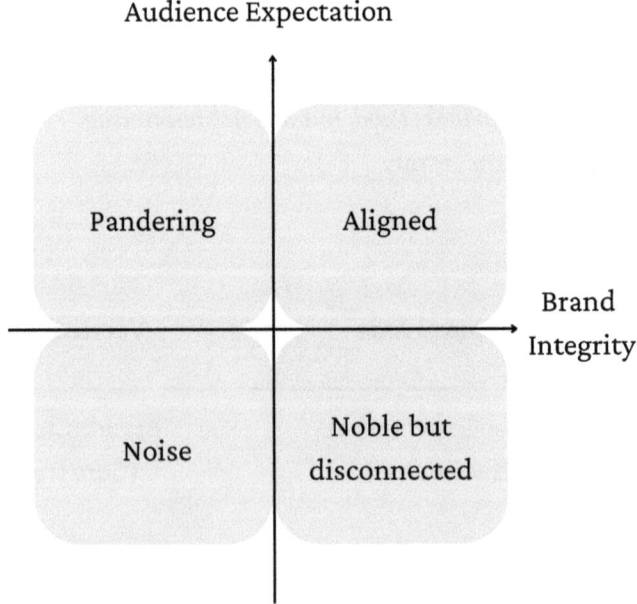

When to Use a 2x2 Frame

Not all tensions are meant to be solved immediately.
Some are meant to be understood. Slowly, sideways, and in layers. That's where a 2x2 grid comes in. A space to explore what happens when opposing truths meet. The axis you choose can reveal so much, whether at the end, the middle, or anywhere along each axis.
These axis pairs work especially well. For example, when creative clarity meets collective pressure. Or when you're torn between your own sense of direction and the expectations of a team, client, or partner. Or when you're trying to preserve the spark of originality, without losing alignment.

Let's imagine a scenario where you're energized by vision but exhausted by execution. The big picture excites you, but day-to-day reality feels heavy. Your ambition still burns, but your capacity feels fragile. The 2x2 in this case might be helpful in gaining perspective that carries you day to day. Here, you could try a Vision vs. Capacity frame or Excitement vs. Sustainability.

Another example. Let's say you're sensing that your intuition is not in alignment with a decision at work or at home. You feel something is off, but can't yet articulate it in the language of strategy or logic. You need a structure that can hold instinct and insight.
Try: Strategy vs. Emotion
Or: Known vs. Felt

When your values quietly clash with outside expectations
You're playing a role that no longer fits. Or maybe you're being asked to deliver something that doesn't align with what you truly believe in.
Try: Personal Beliefs vs. External Expectations
Or: Integrity vs. Impact

Let your tension guide your frame.

You don't have to get it perfect. You just need to get it real enough to start seeing from a new angle. Like the rest of Flow Theory, 2x2 isn't about being right. It's about being real. Seeing clearly enough to shape what you sensed, so you can arrive with quiet conviction. Some frames might not work. That's not failure, it is movement. Every attempt is a rehearsal for clarity.

Build Your Own 2x2
Go back to your highest-scoring mind map branch. What feels like the tension at play?
Try naming two forces that pull in different directions based on your current tension.
No need to get it perfect. Just see what shows up.
Put one on the horizontal, the other on the vertical. Then play. Move your idea, your question, your project through the four quadrants. Watch how clarity begins to take shape, not because you force it, but because you give it space to move.

Framing Tool 5: The "What If..." Flip

One of the quickest ways to break through mental stagnation is to ask a question that bends reality, just enough to let something new in.

"What if the opposite were true?"
"What if this wasn't a problem but a portal?"
"What if I'm not stuck but protecting something I care about?"

These reframes don't need to be logical. They need to be liberating. They momentarily suspend the rules of the game so your imagination can walk freely.

By the time you've mapped your emotional terrain, clarified your language, tried multiple lenses, and explored key tensions, you might feel like you've seen it all.
But the brain loves patterns. And patterns, left unchallenged, become traps.
The "What If..." Flip interrupts your default thinking.
It's like turning the Rubik's Cube of your problem one more time and seeing a side you hadn't noticed before.

Ask yourself "what if..." questions that challenge or contradict your emotional state so you can break its logic and see it differently.
Remember, framing is not only about describing the emotional cue. It's about holding it, confronting it and sometimes flipping it upside down.

Use this frame especially when you have explored every angle, but nothing clicks and when you seek momentum, not necessarily answers.

When you are stuck in self-doubt, looping the same internal story. Or, when you want to challenge assumptions without needing new data, the "What if…" can help you see the terrain differently and it might get you closer to what you are looking for.

Here are some of my personal "What if" flips I like to use in a variety of occasions:

"What if I already have everything I need, but I'm not using it fully?"
"What if this project is waiting for me to be bolder?"
"What if this isn't the wrong path but just the wrong pace?"
"What if the tension isn't a block, but a boundary I'm afraid to cross?"
"What if I'm not confused, I'm just early?"

This Frame is about permission.
It isn't about fantasy, it is about possibility. It creates just enough looseness in the system for clarity to sneak in and it operates with the idea that sometimes, your next insight isn't hidden in the data. It's hiding behind a thought you haven't dared to think yet.

The Courage to Frame

By now, you've done something powerful most people never take the time or emotional energy to do:

You've sat with a tension. You've mapped its terrain.
You've experimented with how to hold it, shape it, and look at it differently.
You've played with metaphor. You've shifted your language.
You've reframed your questions and drew new dimensions with structure.
And maybe, just maybe, you flipped a mental switch with a single "What if..."

Framing isn't about arriving at a conclusion. All of these steps mean you had the courage and the dedication to deal with an ambiguous emotional cue and you managed to look at it from different perspectives giving it enough shape to move forward.
Enough space to feel momentum.
Enough language to feel less alone inside the problem.

When a frame works, you'll feel it.
Not like a puzzle solved but like a breath released.
A subtle internal click that makes the next step feel possible.

That's the role of the frame in Flow Theory:
Not to replace your intuition but to support it.
Not to deliver certainty but to invite motion. And when that motion arrives, when the pressure feels lighter, when the vision starts forming, you're no longer just sensing or shaping.

You're beginning to arrive.

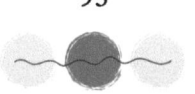

Part III Arrive

What Arrival Can Feel Like

There's a reason people say, "I need to sleep on it."
Sometimes, your clearest thoughts arrive when you stop
thinking.
You feel it in your body. A sense of peace, or readiness.
A weight lifted from your shoulders. A deep breath that feels
like relief.
Other times, it is a wordless knowing that wakes you at 3 a.m.
Or a subtle emotional shift after a nap or walk.
You were tense. Now you're not. You were looping. Now
something has clicked.
These moments are quiet. There is no big announcement.
But suddenly, you know what to do. Or at least, what matters.

I call this arrival. Arrival is the sensation that something inside
you has settled. That the tension has shifted into direction.
That the energy, once swirling in confusion, is now pointing
forward. It may not be loud. But it feels unmistakably real. You
might still be unsure of the final outcome. But the fog has lifted
just enough for the next step to appear.
It's the "yes" you feel in your chest. The breath that drops lower
into your lungs. The weight that lifts, even if the circumstances
haven't changed.

Arrival is not a finish line, it is a starting point that feels like
yours.

Forms of Knowing

Not every arrival feels the same.
Clarity wears many faces. And the way you experience it,
through your mind, body, or heart, is as unique as the journey
that brought you here.
Some arrivals are loud.
A sudden "aha", a phrase that completes the puzzle, or a shift in
direction so clear it demands immediate action.
Others are quiet. A deep breath. A loosened grip. The first good
night of sleep in weeks. These are all valid forms of knowing.

What's important is not the size of the realization, but the felt
sense that something has shifted inside you. You might notice a
wordless confidence replacing the swirl of doubt. Or a single
sentence that crystallizes what was once chaotic. Even a
physical release. Your chest feels lighter, your breath deeper.
A story you've told yourself suddenly no longer makes sense
and a new one begins to form. A tiny next step that feels
unreasonably clear. Still, clarity doesn't always come as a
conclusion. Sometimes, it arrives as permission.
Permission to stop searching and to start creating.
To trust the new rhythm forming within you.

You're not done but you're aligned.
Whatever it is, it wasn't there before but it is now.
Its presence feels unmistakably real.
That is what it feels like to arrive at emotional clarity within the
Flow Theory. And from here, you move forward differently.

Arrival isn't the end of the journey.
It's the moment something new begins to take shape.
You don't have to act immediately.
But you do have to notice.
This is the moment the internal begins to lean outward.
The moment clarity becomes movement. And now that
something has landed, we begin to explore how to carry it
forward.

Tools for Integration

Arrival is more emotional than intellectual. It's a felt shift that is subtle, internal, and often hard to articulate.
But just because it begins in emotion doesn't mean we can't work with it. The clarity you reach in this stage may be quiet, but it is real.
And with the right tools, you can recognize it, stabilize it, and start moving with it.
These tools don't force action or over-analyze the moment.
They help you hold the clarity long enough for it to grow roots and each one supports a different emotional need.

Here are some tools you might find useful in your Flow:

1. Recognition: To name what you've felt.
2. Integration: To connect it to your world.
3. Gentle Action: To respond without pressure.

Use one, or use all. Return to them as needed.
Because once you've arrived, even if only partially, the way forward begins to reveal itself. Let us now have a closer look at each one of these tools and dive a bit deeper into each one.

We start with the *Recognition Tool*.

Clarity can be quiet. It can whisper instead of roar.

That's why the first step after arrival is to recognize what's actually shifted inside you. This is not about explaining it to others. It's about becoming familiar with the shape of your own insight.

Sometimes the shift is a sentence.

Sometimes it's an image.

Sometimes it is a sensation in the body that tells you:

"Something has changed." This tool helps you put that shift into words or at least into form.

Try this:

Write down one sentence that feels new.

Even if it is incomplete. Even if it feels strange.

Example: "I don't want to keep proving myself like this."

Give the insight a name or image.

What would you call this clarity if it were a place, a color, or a symbol?

Example: "It feels like a small flame I want to protect."

Describe the before and after.

"Before I felt ____. Now I feel ____."

Don't explain, just notice.

These acts of recognition give your insight shape.

And once it has shape, it becomes easier to keep.

Recognition is the first spark that tells you something inside has shifted. You have arrived, at least partially, into clarity. Now it is time to live into what you have recognized and that is what *integration* invites you to do.

Integration is the act of folding that spark into your world. You have seen something. Now you begin to carry it with you.This is not about action just yet. It is about alignment.

The goal of integration is not to do more.

It is to do it with intention.

Identify one place in your day-to-day life where this insight already exists. You might be living parts of your clarity already, just unconsciously.

Let that recognition shape one small decision.

Do not overhaul your life. Begin with a step that reflects the shift.

To make it more tangible, here are some ways integration might show up in practice:

I feel most like myself when I'm writing alone. That space already gives me my clarity. Or if I no longer want to prove myself, I may stop saying yes to certain projects. Or I block two hours for a project that excites me, even if no one asked for it.

When you recognize a spark or an insight, ask:

"If this were true, what would change?"

Not what should change.

What would naturally shift if you let it?

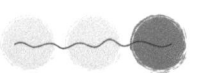

Arrival offers a felt shift but left unattended, even the clearest insight can fade.

Gentle action doesn't mean rushing. It means respecting the clarity that's arrived by giving it a shape it can grow into. This isn't a productivity push.

It's a gesture of care. You're not executing a plan, you're welcoming the insight into your next steps.

Make it small, but sacred.

Choose one meaningful step. Make it real.

Anchor the action emotionally.

Don't just plan what to do. Remind yourself why it matters.

The goal is not to 'finish', but to move in flow with what's now clear.

Try this:

Name a step you'd like to take. Not to fix, but to continue.

Ask: *"What feels obvious now that didn't before?"*

Then: *"What's one action that aligns with that?"*

Book a coffee with someone you need to talk to. Clear your weekend for writing. Make the call you've been avoiding.

Before We Close This Chapter

I have used the Flow Theory in all kinds of situations. To create a business case. To prepare for a job interview. Even to deal with my dad bod. I have offered it to a loved one who had stage fright.

Point is, these were not extraordinary moments. They were human ones. And Flow helped me move through them, not by giving me the answers, but by helping me see the shape of the space I was standing in. And that is the realization I want to share.

Once you begin to recognize the shape of Flow, something changes. It is not that you gain power, or speed, or certainty. What you gain is awareness. A kind of meta awareness.

You begin to see how your mind moves. How your questions evolve. And you start noticing the difference between being inside the experience and walking alongside it with a quiet clarity.

That shift changes how you hold the world.
It changes how you hold yourself. In other words, once you know of the Flow, you can't unsee it.

You have now moved through the full rhythm of Flow.
You have sensed something subtle but real.
You have framed it from multiple angles.
And you have arrived. Not at a final answer, but at a deeper kind of clarity. One that feels internal, emotional, and quietly true.

But just like clarity can take many forms, Flow itself refuses to follow a straight line. It moves in loops. It deepens in layers. And just when you think you have reached a resolution, something new emerges.

You might sense another tension rising just as you begin to feel settled. You might find that framing reveals a new discomfort before you have time to arrive. Or that your moment of clarity unlocks something unexpected underneath it.
This is not a flaw. *This is the nature of Flow.*
And before we close this chapter, there is one final idea we need to explore. It is not a new tool. It is a new understanding. One that speaks not to what you do with Flow, but how it lives with you.

Because this journey, if you stay open to it, never really ends.

The Fractal Nature of Flow

What if the shape of clarity isn't a straight line?
What if it spirals, folds, and repeats?
Flow is not a one-time journey from confusion to insight.
It's a rhythm that repeats itself at different scales, offering a
deeper version of the same movement each time:

Sense. Frame. Arrive.

Sometimes that cycle plays out over weeks.
Sometimes it happens in minutes.
And sometimes, within one stage, a smaller loop begins again.
You might be in Frame, and suddenly sense a new tension. You
might Arrive at clarity, only to realize a *deeper* framing is
needed.
Or you might Sense something subtle, and before naming it,
you're already experiencing a moment of arrival.

This is what makes Flow fractal.
It repeats within itself. Like patterns in nature, spirals in
seashells, or the branching of trees. Each part contains the
whole. Each moment holds the possibility of deeper
understanding.
And this is why it is okay if your journey through Flow doesn't
feel linear.
It isn't.

Flow doesn't move like a staircase, it moves like a spiral.

With every loop, you're not repeating, you're refining.

This is the truth that quiets the inner critic.

You're not stuck.

You're circling closer to something meaningful.

You're not going backward.

You're returning with greater depth, sharper clarity, and a gentler presence.

So as you leave these pages behind and move back into your own life, know this:

Flow doesn't end here.

It begins again.

Each time you decide to listen.

Part IV
Living the Flow Theory

I was so focused on getting through that door that I thought
everything began and ended with the door itself.
And that was my mistake.

Misfires and Loops

The Flow Theory is an emotional endeavor.
It requires looking at your emotional cues as honestly and non-judgmentally as possible and staying with them long enough for something to emerge. That's often easier said than done. And it often takes longer than we expect.
The combination of uncomfortable internal confrontation and the time it takes for an emotional cue to reveal its underlying tension or signal creates the perfect environment for missteps or for shortcuts taken unknowingly.

Once the Flow Theory became clear in my mind and I began using it daily, I realized how often, in the past, I had gotten stuck in the Sense stage or carried vague, unfiltered cues all the way through.
I tried to build frames shaped by uncertainty, ego, or emotional fog. The result? Exhaustion. Loss of analytical sharpness. The feeling of searching for a key to a door that might not even lead where you want to go.

Not every attempt to apply the Flow Theory goes smoothly and it might feel confusing at the beginning. You might follow the wrong cues and frame them the way it feels right not necessarily the way it should be and you might end up with a wrong feeling of arrival. I have been through this and there are ways you can avoid misfires from happening.
This is what this part of the book will take you through.

Sometimes we rush into Frame without truly sensing. Sometimes we might mistake a mental workaround for a meaningful reframe. Other times we push for clarity because we're tired of discomfort and what we find isn't clarity at all, just cognitive closure dressed up as insight.

These aren't failures. They're misfires and they're part of living the Flow. A misfire happens when we move too quickly, or too rigidly, through the process.
When we cling to the first metaphor that makes us feel smart. When we use language as a shield instead of an invitation. Or when we loop through tools without listening for what's real. And often, when this happens, we find ourselves back where we started, confused, restless, or more doubtful than before.

But looping is not the opposite of progress.
It's the Flow letting you know something deeper is still speaking and asking for a different kind of attention.

Living the Flow Theory means developing the sensitivity to notice these loops. Not with frustration, but with curiosity. It means realizing the door was never the point.
What matters is the readiness with which you walk through it and whether the path beyond still feels like yours.

The Sense Health Check

When Flow breaks down, it often starts in the Sense stage. Not because we didn't feel something, but because we didn't give it time, space, or attention. We moved too fast. We forced clarity. Or we ignored the emotional cue because we didn't trust it or couldn't name it. You can't build a frame around something you haven't truly felt.

The Sense stage is about tuning in, not solving. But when we're tired, under pressure, or eager to move forward, we often bypass it or we confuse mental restlessness with emotional recognition.
Here's how to check whether your sensing was truly sensing.

Ask Yourself:
Did I slow down enough to notice what I'm actually feeling or did I name it too quickly?
Was I listening to my intuition, or to my assumptions?
Did I sit with the emotional cue long enough to distinguish whether it was a tension or a signal?
Have I tried to map where the feeling lives before I've explored what it wants?
Did I skip from discomfort straight into fixing?

If your sensing feels rushed or vague, return to the moment that felt charged.
Don't analyze. Just feel it again.

Clarity doesn't occur because you push harder.
It happens when you slow down long enough to notice it has been there all along.
Here are some common misfires to keep in mind when exploring your emotional cues:

There are some common misfires to keep in mind when exploring your emotional cues. Sometimes, we mistake urgency for clarity and feel compelled to act quickly before we have truly understood what we are sensing. Other times, we rush to name a feeling too soon and end up calling it the wrong thing, which can lead us further away from what is really going on. Emotional exhaustion can easily masquerade as insight, especially when we are desperate for relief and any answer feels like the right one. And perhaps most often, we treat ambiguity as a flaw to eliminate rather than what it often is, a message to interpret, slowly and with care.

Understanding the importance of clarity at this stage helps you pursue solutions that address the true ambiguity, rather than rushing toward an incomplete or misdirected fix.

The Frame Health Check

Framing is where we begin to shape our tension or signal and where we give it a lens, a metaphor, a question, or a structure. The right frame might not make the problem easier. It does, however, make it clearer.

But frames are only as effective as the clarity they're built on. And when we apply them too quickly, too rigidly, or too cleverly, they stop helping us see and start helping us avoid.

When Flow breaks down in the Frame stage, it is often not because the tools didn't work. It's because we weren't ready to use them or we used them to manage our discomfort, rather than to understand it.

Framing only works when it holds truth, not when it hides what we're not ready to name.

Ask Yourself:

Did I create this frame too early? Before the emotional cue had time to clarify?

Does the metaphor or structure I used feel emotionally resonant or just conceptually sharp?

Am I using tools to make sense or to escape something I don't want to feel?

Did I frame the clearest tension, or the one I felt most comfortable addressing?

Does the frame open something or shut something down?

When your framing feels smart but somehow disconnected, return to what it was meant to hold.

Don't defend it. Just look again.

You could probe and search for misfires. These could be choosing a metaphor that sounds good but doesn't feel true. Or you might find out you have been framing the wrong part of the problem because it is easier.

Using language to impress or protect, instead of reveal could be another framing misfire.

Another example is forcing structure onto something that's still unfolding or turning clarity into closure too soon.

Understanding when your frame is carrying your insight and when it is obscuring it, is one of the hardest and most important parts of Flow.

Because a strong frame doesn't wrap things up.

It holds them in place, until you're ready to arrive.

The Arrive Alignment Check

Arrive is not the reward. It's the recognition. And in my experience, arriving rarely feels cinematic or euphoric.
It lives deeper than that.
Sometimes, it is finally coming to terms with an outcome you didn't want to accept.
Sometimes, it is a subtle "aha."
It is the quiet acceptance of what's ahead, because now, you see it clearly. Or it might come as a powerful realization or a soft release.

Whatever shape it takes, Arrive offers two things above all: clarity and closure.
Arriving is the emotional outcome of facing what was vague, heavy, or hard to hold.
It is what happens when you've done the work of listening, framing, and staying.
To arrive is to unlock the door and look behind it.
And what you find may not be what you expected.
That's not a failure. *That's the point.*

Arrive isn't there to give you what you wanted.
It's there to show you what's real so you can finally move.

Similar to the other Flow states, it is important not to mistake the clarity that comes with arrive.

Ask Yourself:

Does this feel like relief or like resistance?

Is this what I hoped would happen, or what now feels true?

Do I feel a quiet shift in my body, even if my mind still has questions?

Is the weight I was carrying gone or has it simply changed shape?

Can I sense a readiness to begin even if I don't yet know what comes next?

Arrival is not the celebration. It is the alignment.

It is a felt sense that you have seen what needed to be seen, and now you can move differently. But even in this stage, it is easy to misread the moment. We mistake momentary excitement for emotional clarity and rush ahead without grounding the insight. We force closure simply because we are tired of not knowing, and any answer feels better than the weight of ambiguity. We might chase a perfect insight when a quiet and simple truth is already waiting. We might expect euphoria when what we truly need is peace. And often, we confuse motion for momentum, forgetting that not all movement means progress.

This is how misfires at the Arrive stage might look.

Part V
The Flow Toolkit

Using the Flow Theory in Practice

You do not need to fully understand The Flow Theory to benefit from it. Even if you have never heard of it before now, you can still tap into its rhythm. The rhythm of noticing your emotional cues, letting them surface, and giving them space to breathe. Clarity often follows.

In other words, you can use The Flow Theory without becoming deeply involved in its structure. You do not need to memorize stages or tools. You only need to be present with what you feel and allow it to guide your attention.

Over time, I have developed my own Flow toolkit. Diaries, checklists, mind maps, and even AI prompts have helped me navigate moments of uncertainty. I have set up rituals and systems, including calendar routines, with Flow Theory at their core. They have served me well.

In this chapter, I will share some of those tools. Not as prescriptions, but as possibilities. You may find them useful, or you might be inspired to create your own.
As your own version of The Flow Theory begins to take shape, your tools will shape with it.

The Flow Diary or Weekly Check-In

Emotional clarity is cumulative. If you do not capture it, it fades. This is how I use the Flow Theory continuously in my own life, and I am sharing it in case it resonates with others navigating their own emotional landscapes.

Over time, I came to realize how easily we forget emotional cues. Even worse, we tend to mislabel them. Often this happens simply because we do not give them enough mindful attention. Left unacknowledged, these cues tend to intensify and return as stress, frustration, or disconnection.
That is why I pay attention to emotional cues and treat them like data points.

Once a week, I spend 30 quiet minutes capturing what I have felt, noticed, or sensed. I do not try to solve anything immediately. I simply collect, revisit, and reflect. By doing this consistently, I have become better equipped to face uncertainty and more attuned to my surroundings. I move through daily life with greater awareness.

You can apply this in your work or personal life. The principle is the same: collect emotional cues, no matter how small, and stay aware of what is unfolding.
Let me show you how.

A Flow Diary Example

Collect Emotional Cues

Write down the moments that stood out emotionally, however small. A heaviness before a meeting. A burst of joy during a conversation. A recurring frustration. A quiet dread.

Label Them Gently

Don't force interpretation. Just ask: Was this a tension? Or a signal?
Write a few words beside each to capture what it felt like, without judgment.

Reflect & Pattern

Look over your list. Do certain feelings repeat? Do they cluster around the same person, situation, or time of day?
What are you sensing, now that you see them together?

Frame a Question

Choose one or two cues that feel emotionally charged. Don't try to fix them, just shape them into framing questions.
"What is this frustration trying to protect?"
"What am I not saying out loud?"

Name One Arrival or Next Step
Has anything shifted, even slightly?
Is there one insight, action, or release you can name?
You don't need to act. You just need to notice.

This is not a journal. It's not a to-do list.
It's a *mirror for your emotional intelligence.* A space to watch Flow unfold over time.

You don't need to do this perfectly. You just need to do it regularly. Because *clarity compounds.* And your cues are speaking. Even if softly.

Flow Theory Based LLM AI Prompts

The Flow Theory can be used with large language models (like ChatGPT) as a companion to your thinking process. You can guide the AI to mirror the Flow Theory structure: from sensing, to framing, to arriving.

Since the Flow is a mental exercise, you can benefit from AI to play the sparring partner for you and help you navigate your emotional cues and thought process while keeping you within the Flow. In this part of the book, I offer some examples of how you can use the Flow Theory with AI on demand through a series of prompts.

Flow prompts are , unlike what you might be used to or have heard of, not about getting an answer immediately. They train your AI to gently accompany you through a flow cycle and help you gain clarity without rushing into conclusions. I have offered some of these prompts to people who have never used AI before in languages I can not speak and yet the results have been consistent with a deep intellectual discovery session unfolding emotional cues and a clarity that was not imaginable before.

You can use these prompts when you're feeling stuck, uncertain, or when you're on the edge of something important but unclear. Copy, paste, and adapt as needed.

1-Full Flow Theory Process Prompt

Purpose: Guide an LLM through the entire Flow Theory rhythm: Sense, Frame, Arrive
Use when: You are feeling emotionally unclear, stuck, or in a quiet state of inner questioning
Prompt:
I want to think through something using The Flow Theory.
Please guide me gently through the three stages:

- *Sense: help me slow down and notice emotional cues or inner signals*
- *Frame: help me shift perspectives using questions, metaphors, or reframing language*
- *Arrive: help me sense what is changing inside me, even if it is small*

Move slowly. Ask one question at a time, and wait for me to reflect.
Do not solve the situation. Stay with the feeling.
Help me notice if I am sensing a tension (a feeling of friction) or a signal (a quiet direction).
Let us stay with what is true, not what is finished.

2-Weekly Flow Diary Prompt

Purpose: Capture and reflect on emotional cues from the past week

Use when: Doing a weekly review based on your Flow Diary practice

Prompt:

I want to reflect on my week through the lens of Flow Theory.
Please guide me step by step.
Start by helping me sense:

- *What emotional cues stood out this week?*
- *Which of these feel like tensions? Which feel like signals?*

Then help me frame:

- *Are there recurring patterns or stories I am telling myself?*
- *Can you help me shape one or two framing questions that open something new?*

And finally, help me arrive:

- *Is there a shift I can feel, even if I cannot explain it?*
- *What feels more clear, more grounded, or ready to be moved with?*

Please go slowly. Ask one thing at a time. This is not about finding the answer. It is about meeting what is already there.

3-Signal vs. Tension Sorting Prompt

Purpose: Gently separate emotional cues into those that carry weight and those that carry direction.

Use when: You feel emotionally full or conflicted and want to understand what is pulling you in which direction.

Prompt:

I am noticing a mix of emotions but I cannot yet tell what they are asking of me.

Some feel heavy. Some feel important. Some feel like both.

Please help me sort what I am sensing into two categories:

- *Tensions (feel unresolved, tight, or draining)*
- *Signals (feel energizing, clear, or quietly meaningful)*

Ask me one question at a time.

Help me name what I am feeling, where it sits in my body, and whether it feels like friction or quiet pull.

If I am unsure, help me stay with the uncertainty without rushing to label it. I do not need a solution. I just want to better understand what is asking for my attention, and what is quietly inviting me forward.

4-Frame Diagnosis Prompt

Purpose: Evaluate whether your current way of seeing or describing a problem is helping or hiding
Use when: Something feels slightly off in how you are holding a situation or story
Prompt:
I want to reflect on how I have framed a situation.
Something feels misaligned, and I want to check whether the way I am naming things is helping me or getting in the way.
Please ask me one question at a time. Help me explore gently.
- *Did I name this too early, before I fully sensed it?*
- *Does this metaphor or label feel emotionally true, or just intellectually satisfying?*
- *Is my language bringing me closer to what I feel, or creating distance?*
- *Am I shaping this story to feel safe, or to feel real?*

I do not need to fix the frame. I want to feel whether it fits.
Help me stay with what feels unresolved and explore whether a more honest frame is ready to emerge.

5-Arrive Audit Prompt

Purpose: Help you recognize emotional clarity and begin to live in it without rushing to action

Use when: You feel something has shifted but are unsure what comes next

Prompt:

I think I have reached a moment of clarity, but I want to stay with it a little longer.

I want to be sure I have felt it fully before I move forward.

Please help me reflect on the following:

- *What feels different now, even if it is small?*
- *What truth do I feel ready to accept?*
- *What tension has softened, shifted, or disappeared?*
- *What is one gentle action that would not force anything, but simply honor what I have seen?*

Ask me slowly. Let the clarity stay tender for a moment before I act on it. This is not about doing more. It is about noticing what has changed, and choosing to walk with it.

Part VI
Held, Then Given

Reflection

I set out to make sense of my own mind, and The Flow Theory emerged from that pursuit.
I wanted to understand whether there was a deeper truth behind my gut feelings. Whether the way I think through uncertainty had a pattern. A method. A shape.
I wondered if there was a formula for thinking outside the box.

In time, I realized it is not a formula. It is a practice.
It is the courage to stay with what feels intimidating.
The curiosity to hold it gently. And the patience to question it until the truth it carries reveals itself.

This book is my attempt to map that inner process.
To name it. To offer it. You may find parts of it true for you.
Or you may see ambiguity with new eyes.
Either way, if sharing what goes on in my mind has helped you in some small way, then it was worth it.

It certainly helped me.

Finally, this book is not free of grammatical or linguistic flaws. I am not the typical kind of person who writes a book. I am pragmatic and I value the spark and the journey more than the details. So if you come across the occasional typo or misalignment, I hope you can see past it and find value in the ideas themselves.

Acknowledgements

This book would not exist without the slow, quiet accumulation of conversations, moments, and mentors that shaped how I think and feel about thinking itself.

To my family, especially my wife, for holding space when I needed to wander and for always reminding me where home is.

To friends and collaborators who didn't try to "solve" me, but walked alongside me in ambiguity. Your presence shaped this work more than you know.

To the readers who found this book without knowing what they were looking for: thank you for giving your attention to something that doesn't scream, but calls.

And to the countless thinkers, writers, and artists whose ideas ripple through these pages: I carry your insights like echoes, not citations.

Final Words

This book offers an in-depth journey into the principles behind Flow Theory. A rhythm of sensing, framing, and arriving through ambiguity and doubt. These prompts are not about solving faster.
You can explore more tailored LLM prompts and practical applications by visiting the Flow Theory website and its growing LLM Prompt Library.

Last but not least, if you like to get in touch or share your thoughts and reflections , I would love to hear from you. This was never a monologue and is meant to be shared and reflected on together.

https://www.the-flow-theory.com/

ISBN: 978-3-7693-1503-5

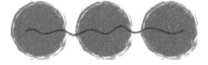